THIS PERSON IS HEALING:

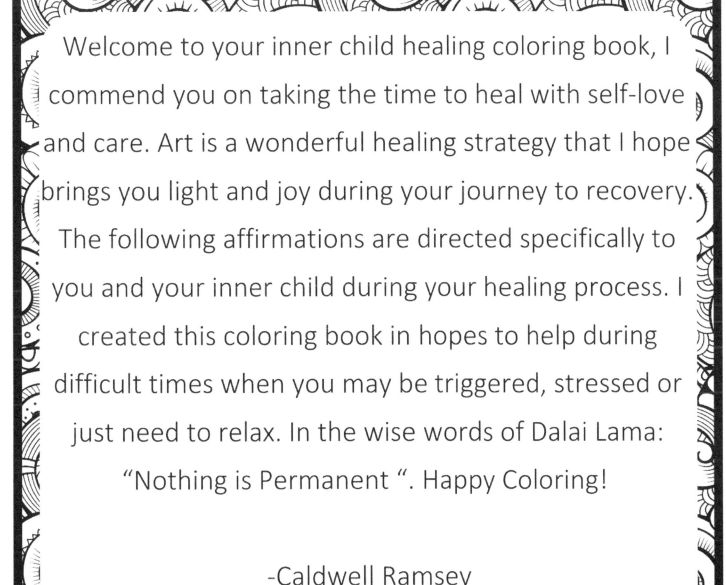

Welcome to your inner child healing coloring book, I commend you on taking the time to heal with self-love and care. Art is a wonderful healing strategy that I hope brings you light and joy during your journey to recovery. The following affirmations are directed specifically to you and your inner child during your healing process. I created this coloring book in hopes to help during difficult times when you may be triggered, stressed or just need to relax. In the wise words of Dalai Lama: "Nothing is Permanent ". Happy Coloring!

-Caldwell Ramsey

Visit CaldwellRamseybooks.com for a complimentary inner child workbook.

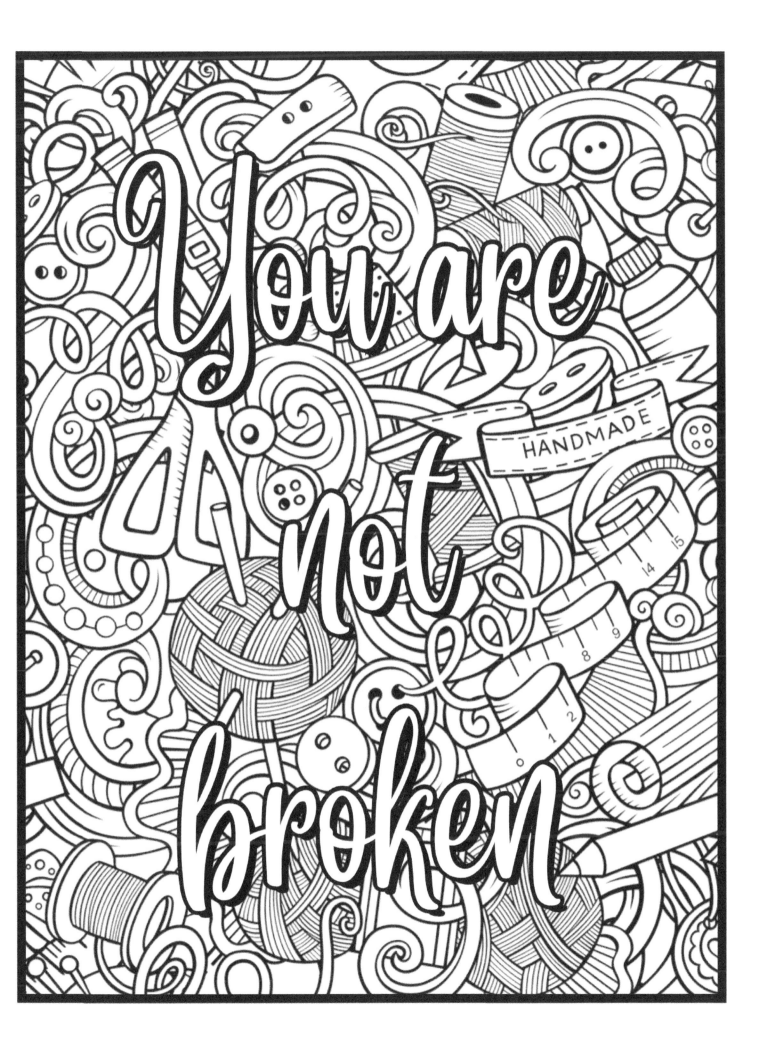

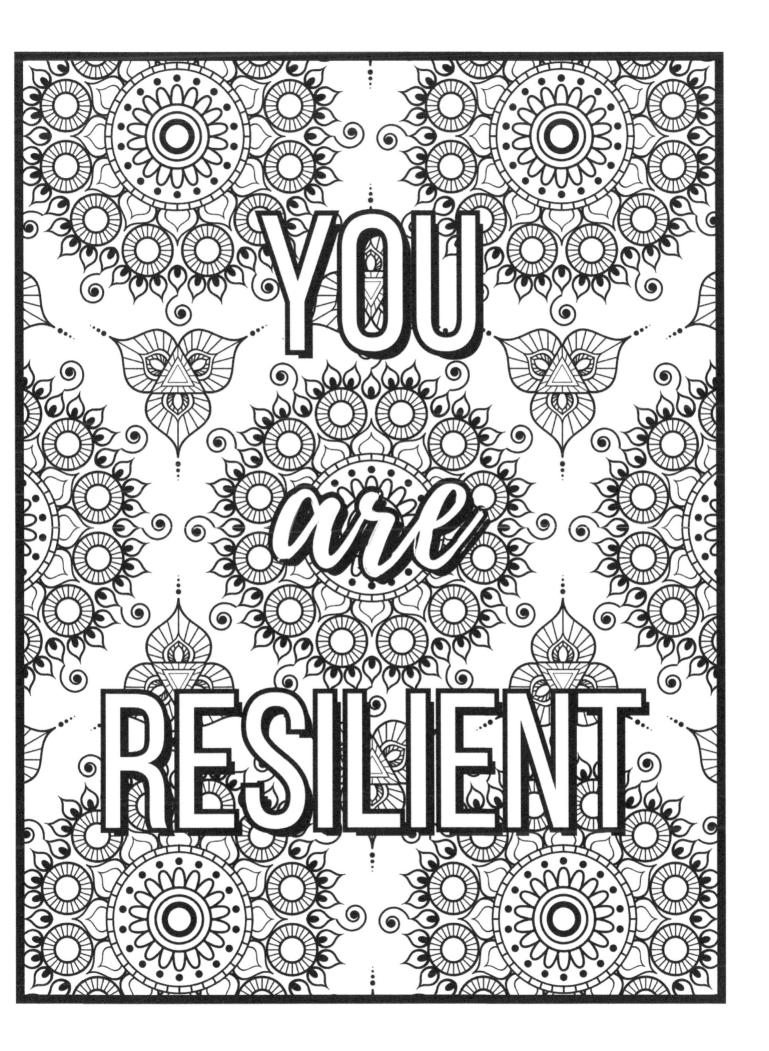

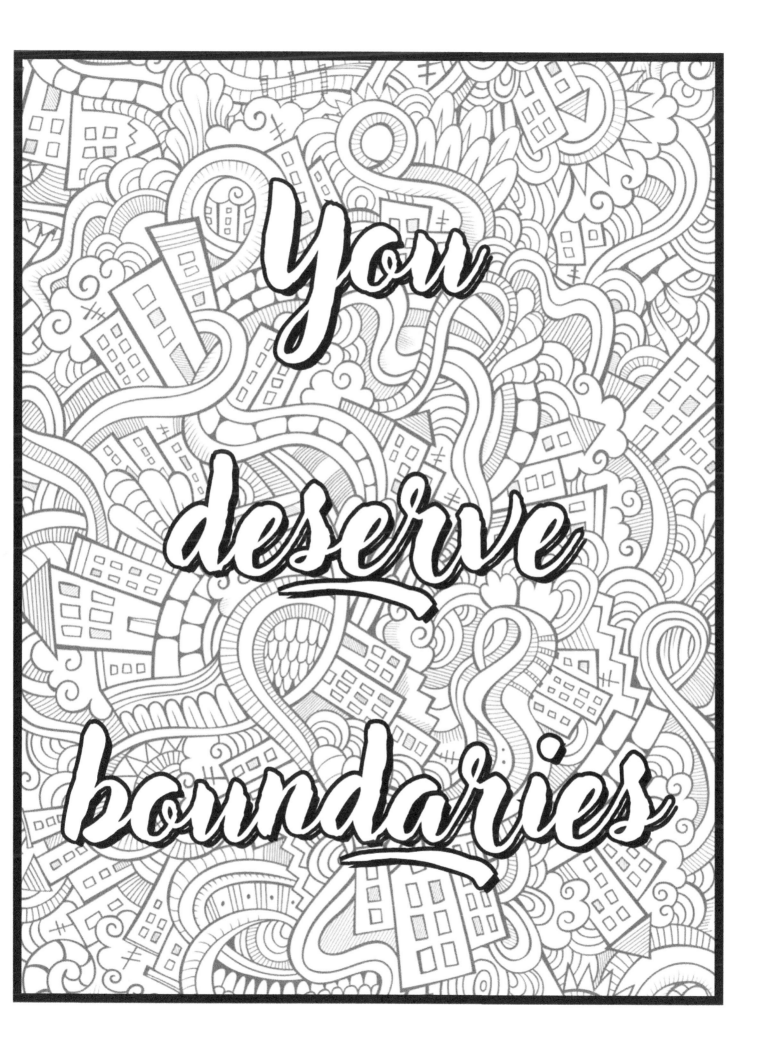

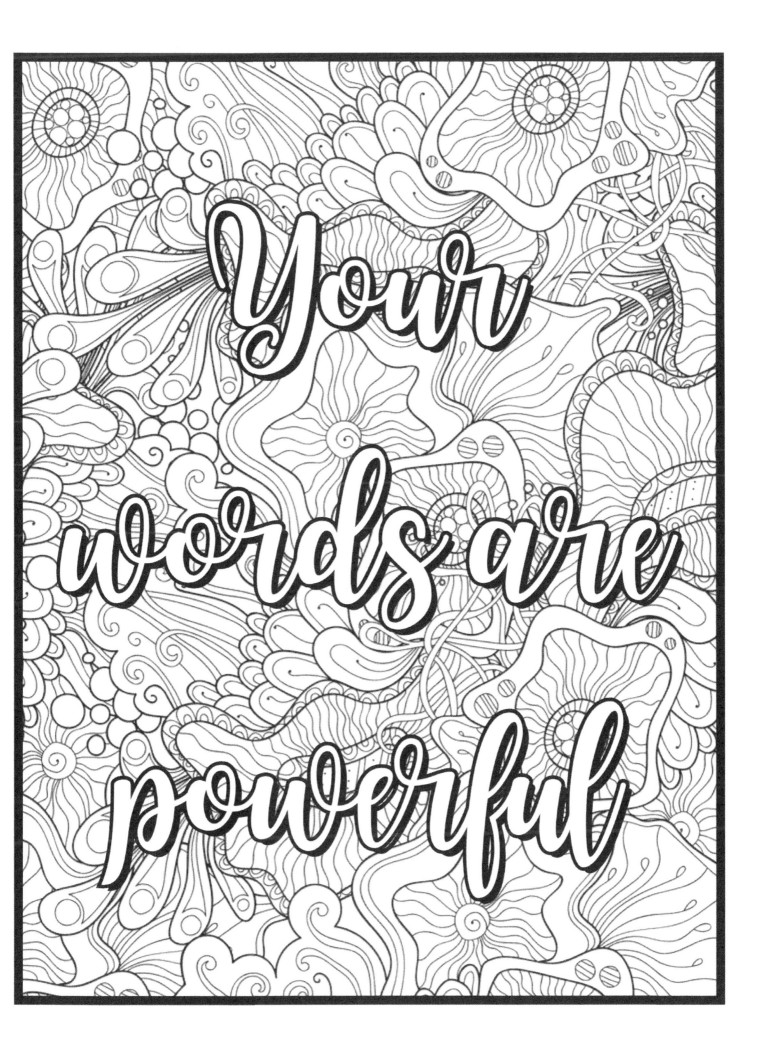

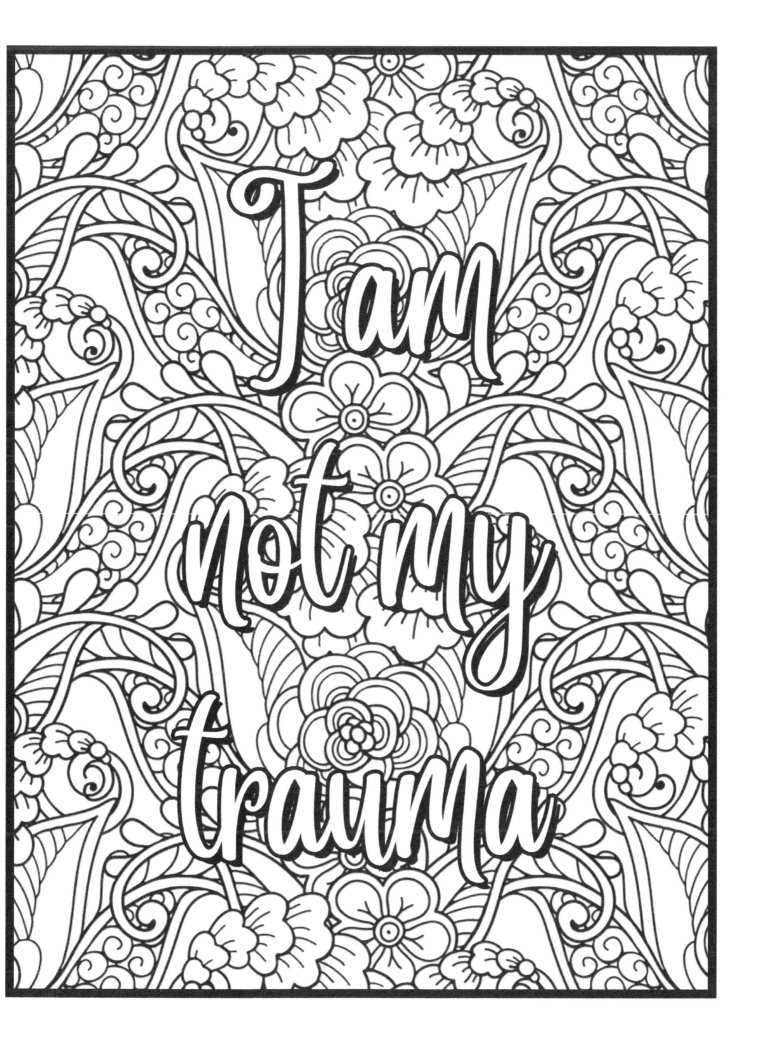

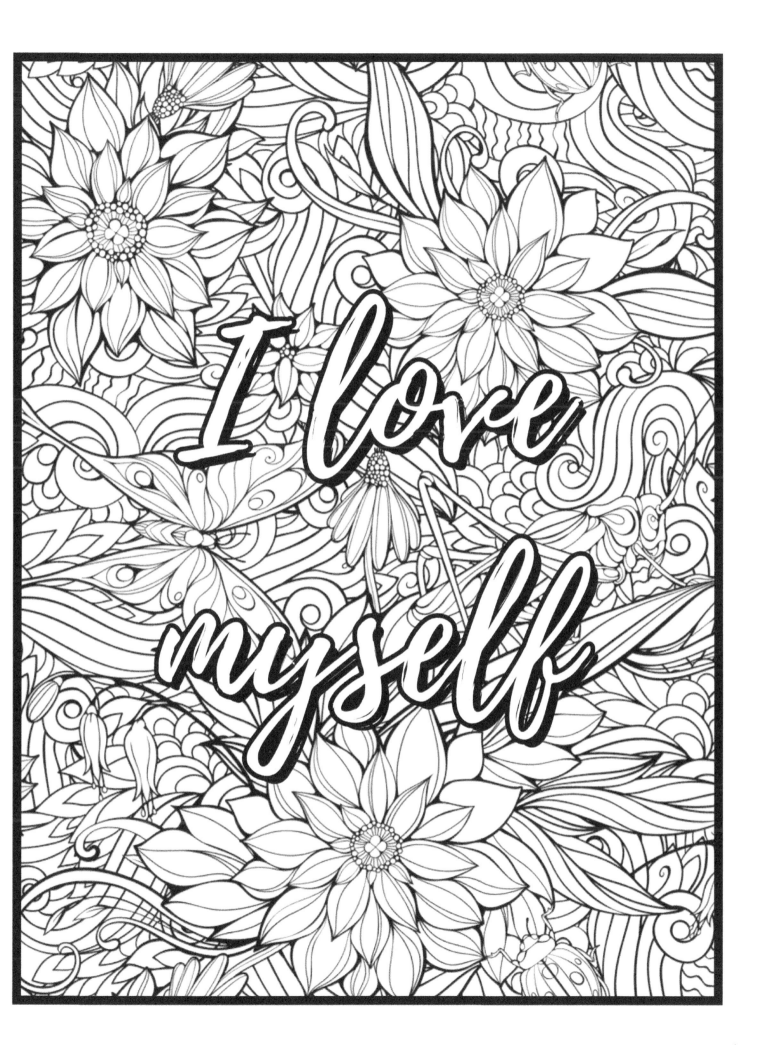

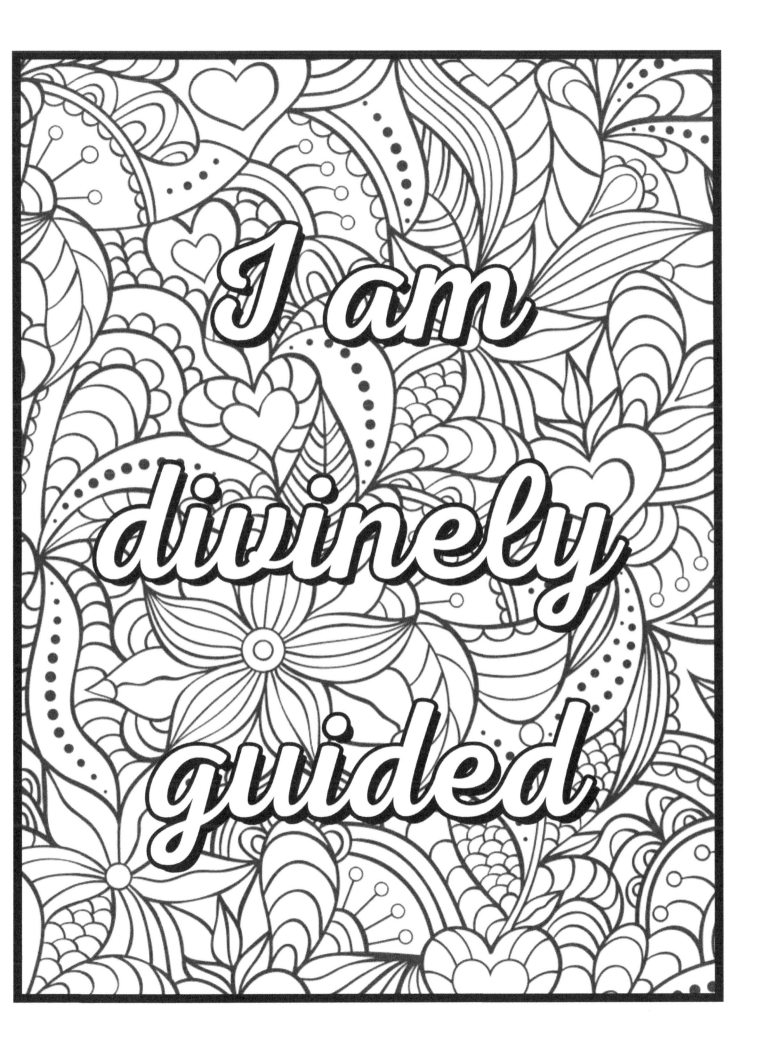

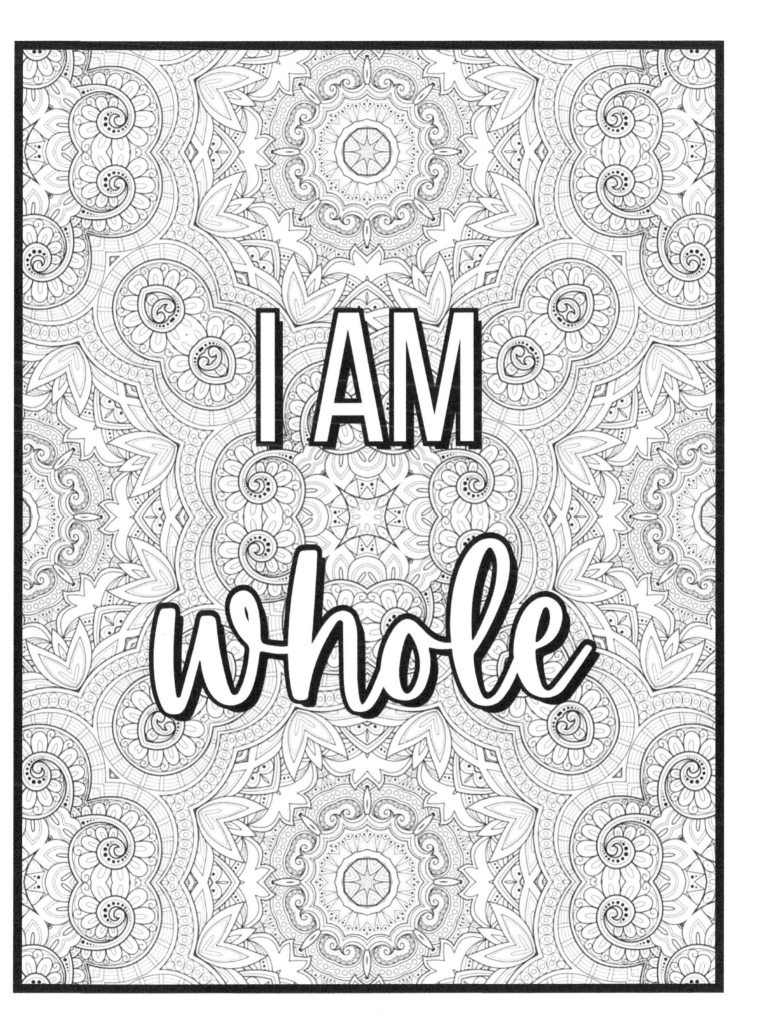

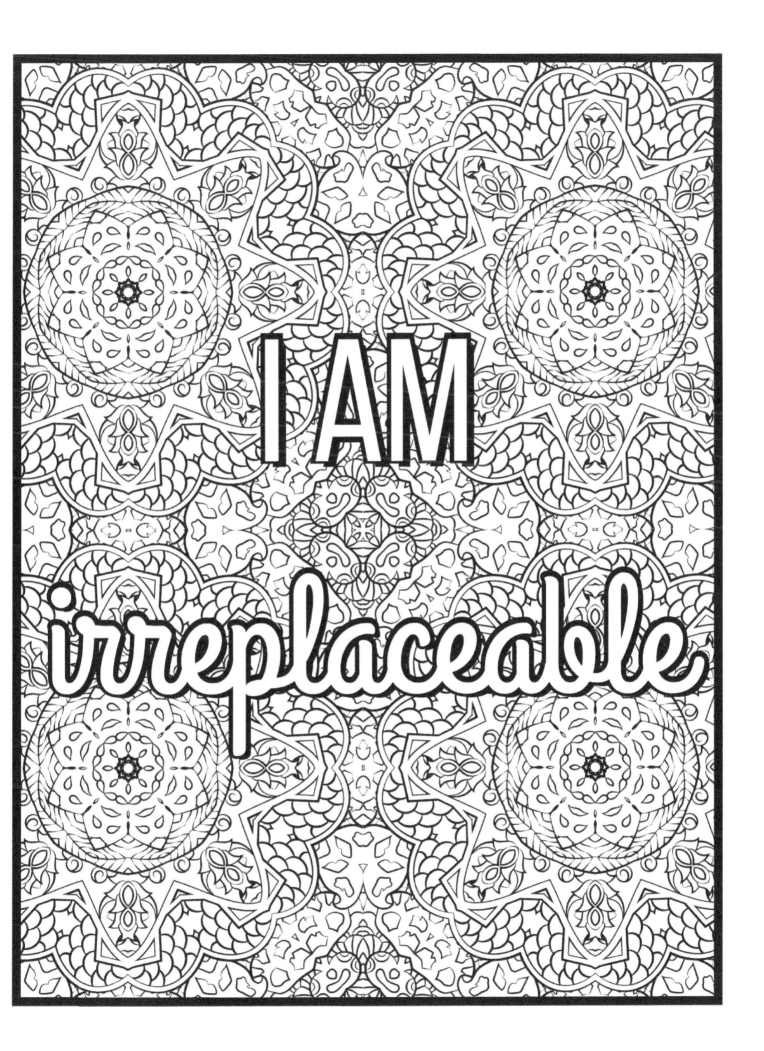

Made in the USA
Las Vegas, NV
01 May 2024

89400748R00070